FIREFIGHTERS
FIGHT FIRES

**This book is dedicated
to the
Webster Groves Fire Department,
Webster Groves, Missouri**

Design and electronic page composition
Lindaanne Donohoe Design

Photo research
Feldman & Associates, Inc.

Picture Acknowledgments

Dembinsky Photo Assoc. — ©Sharon Cummings — 30;
©Marvin L. Dembinsky, Jr. — 11; ©Daniel Dempster— 7;
©DPA — 8, 12, 16, 18, 19, 23, 25, 26, 27; ©Russ Gutshall — 22;
©Dean Helsel — 24; ©Larime Photographic— 3, 17, 21 29;
©David Moore — 15

©Lindaanne Donohoe Design — 9

David R. Frazier Photolibrary — ©David R. Frazier — 10, 14, 20;
©Trent Steffler — 6

©SuperStock, International, Inc. — 13

Visuals Unlimited — ©N. Noyes — cover; ©Emily Stong — 4;
©Glenn Oliver — 5; ©Bob Newman, 28

Library of Congress Cataloging-in-Publication Data

Greene, Carol.

Firefighters fight fires/Carol Greene.
p.   cm.
Includes index.
Summary: Describes what happens when a fire alarm goes off
at a firehouse, from firefighters racing to a fire scene
to the rescue of a cat from a burning building.
ISBN 1-56766-301-X (hardcover)
1. Fire extinction — Juvenile literature. [1. Fire extinction.] I. Title.

TH9148.G73   1996   96-713
628.9'25—dc20   CIP
                                                        AC

FIREFIGHTERS
FIGHT FIRES

By Carol Greene

THE CHILD'S WORLD®

Bzzzzzzzzz!

Goes the fire station buzzer.

Hurry, firefighters.
IT'S A FIRE!

Quickly the firefighters pull on their pants.

Boots too! *ZWOOOP! ZWOOOP!*

They race to their firetrucks.
VROOOMMM! VROOOMMM!

Drivers start the big trucks.
Out they roll.

WOOOEEEE!

The sirens scream.

Get out of the way, everyone.

A house is on fire.
The pumper gets there first.
The firefighters grab a hose.

They connect it to a fire hydrant.
CLICK! CLICK!

Here comes the chief.
The chief tells everyone else what to do.

WOOOOEEEE! WOOOEEEEEE!

Here comes the ladder truck.

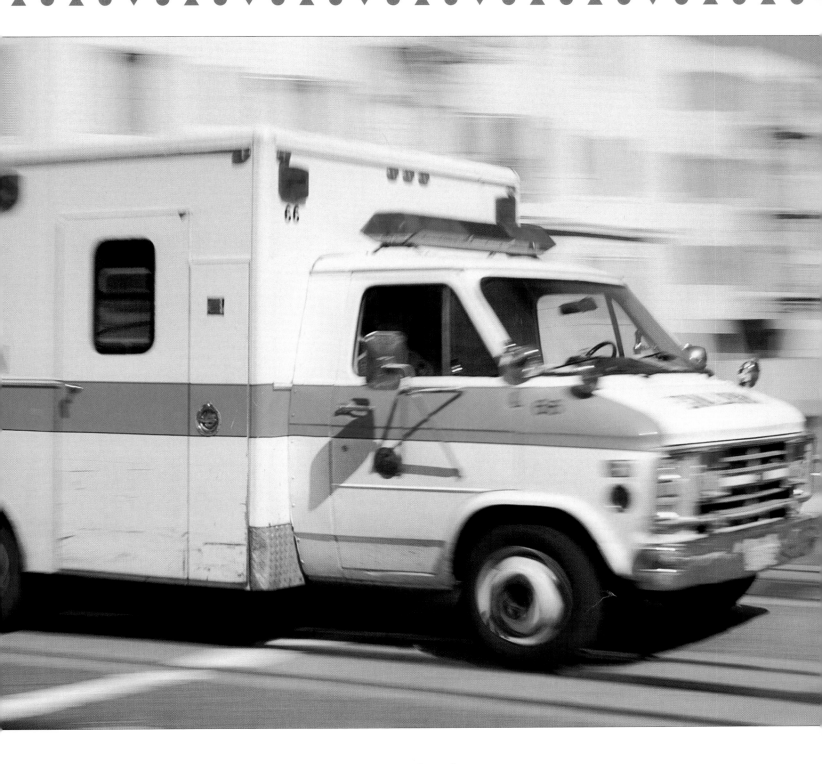

Here comes the ambulance.
Is anyone hurt? No.

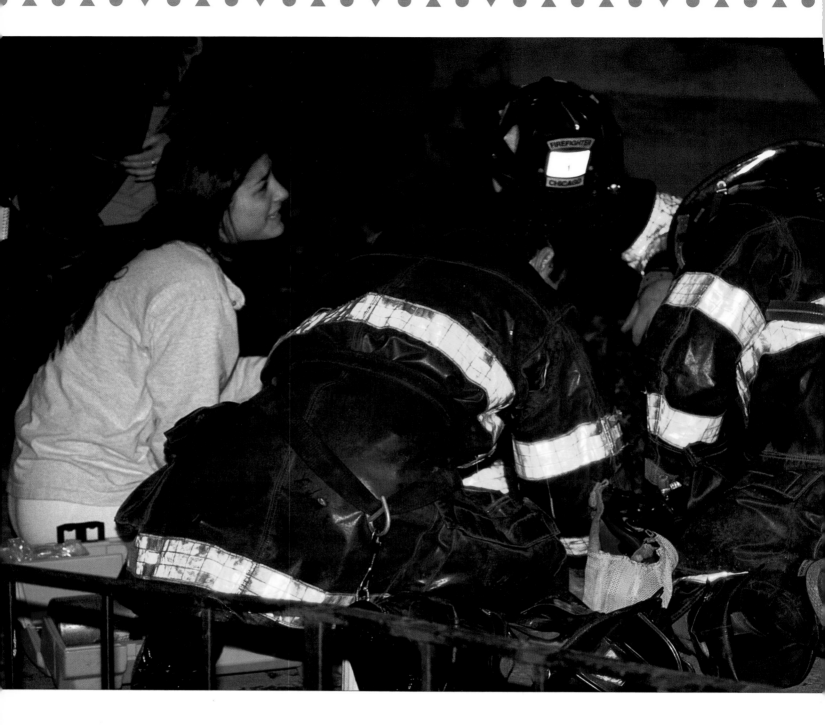

The people heard their smoke alarm.
They got out. Now they are safe.
But their cat is in the house.

BANG! BANG! CRASH!
One firefighter breaks down the back
door. Another goes into the house.

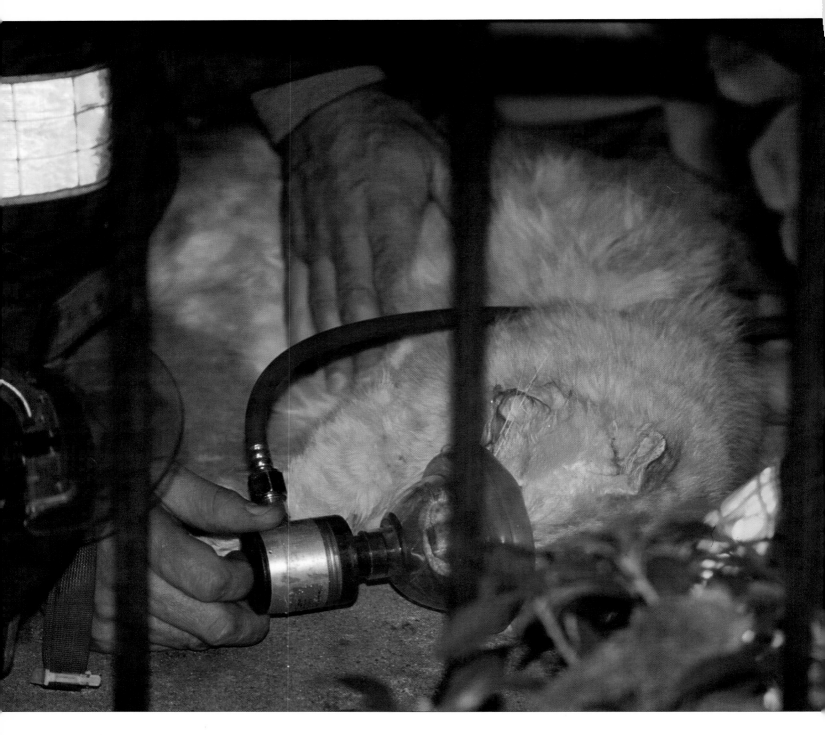

Did they find the cat?
Yes. But is it too late?

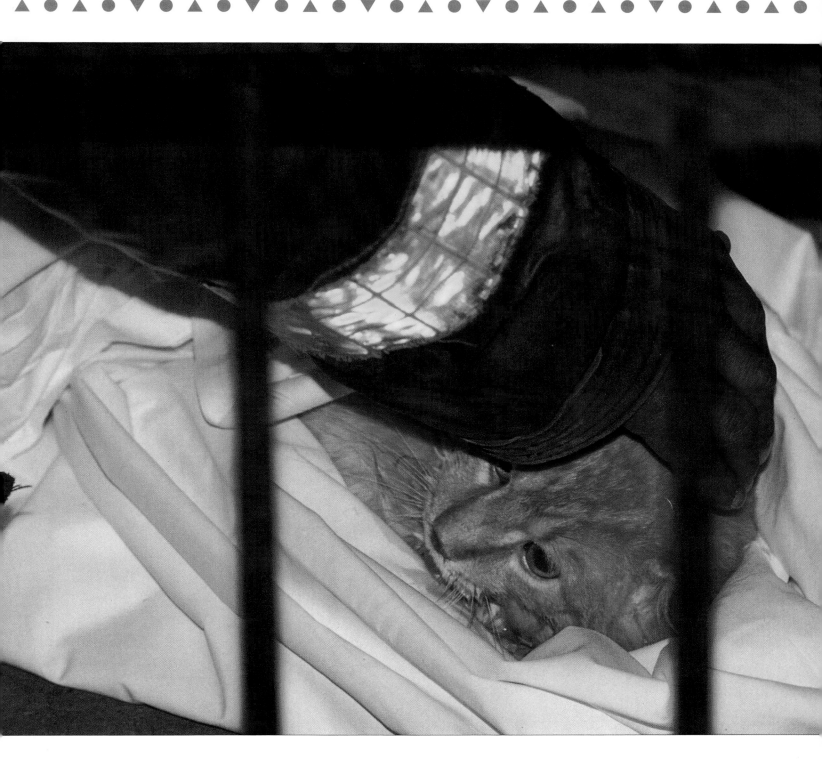

"MEEOWW" says the cat.

"Thank you!" say the owners.

Other firefighters go
into the house with hoses.
PSH-SSSS-SSSSSS!

The water is putting the fire out.
The smoke smells terrible.
YUK!

There goes a firefighter up a ladder.
THUD! THUD! CRASH!

He chops a hole in the roof
to let out more smoke.

Is the fire out?
The firefighters check everywhere.

The fire is out.
The firefighters have done their job.

VROOOMMM! VROOOMMM!
The firefighters
go back to the firehouse.

Right away, they clean
their trucks and equipment.
SWISH! SWISH! SPLASH!

They check the fire hoses.
Firefighters must always be ready.

They never know when the buzzer
will sound. . .

BZZZZZZZ! IT'S A FIRE!

Questions and Answers

What do firefighters do?

Firefighters fight fires. They save lives. They do safety checks to keep fires from startlng. They tell people how to prevent fires.

How do people learn to be firefighters?

Most firefighters go to high school for four years. Then some go to college for two more years. Others go to a fire-fighting school. They all study how fires start, how fires act, and how to put fires out. Firefighters learn a lot from other firefighters too.

What kind of people are firefighters?

Firefighters are people who help people. They are strong. They can carry a person or hold a heavy hose. Firefighters must be healthy. They can work for a long time with no rest.

How much money do firefighters make?

Most firefighters make about $21,000 a year. Some make more than that. Some make less. In some places, firefighters are volunteers. They work for free.

Glossary

pumper truck—a special machine that uses its power to move water from the fire hydrant to the fire hoses

fire hydrant—container for a small pipe that is connected to a big pipe that carries water in cities and towns

chief—the leader of a team of firefighters

ladder truck—a specially made, large, four-wheeled machine that carries ladders and firefighters to fires

ambulance—a special car or van built with special equipment and used to carry sick and wounded people to a hospital

smoke alarm—an object usually powered by batteries that makes a loud sound when smoke hits it

hose—a heavy cloth tube made to carry water from the fire hydrant to the fire

CAROL GREENE has written over 200 books for children. She also likes to read books, make teddy bears, work in her garden, and sing. Ms. Greene lives in Webster Groves, Missouri.